D1604770

Your Mission to Mars

by M. J. Cosson
illustrated by Scott Burroughs

Content Consultant
Diane M. Bollen, Research Scientist,
Cornell University

magic
wagon

visit us at www.abdopublishing.com

Printed in the United States of America, North Mankato, Minnesota.
052011
092011
 THIS BOOK CONTAINS AT LEAST 10% RECYCLED MATERIALS.

Text by M. J. Cosson
Illustrations by Scott Burroughs
Edited by Holly Saari
Design and production by Becky Daum

Library of Congress Cataloging-in-Publication Data
Cosson, M. J.
  Your mission to Mars / by M.J. Cosson ; illustrated by Scott Burroughs.
     p. cm. — (The planets)
  Includes index.
  ISBN 978-1-61641-679-9
  1. Mars (Planet)—Juvenile literature. I. Burroughs, Scott, ill. II. Title.
  QB641.C6845 2012
  523.43—dc22
                            2011006775

Table of Contents

Imagine You Could Go

Have you heard that there might have been life on Mars millions of years ago? Mars is Earth's next-door neighbor. It is like Earth in many ways. For a long time, scientists wondered if plants and animals lived there, too. Now they know there is no life on the planet.

No one has ever gone to Mars. But robots have explored it. Imagine you could go to Mars and see what it's like for yourself.

Scientists have found signs of ancient floods on Mars. They have also found signs of water at icy areas of the planet, both above and below ground.

MERCURY

VENUS

EARTH

MARS

SUN

5

Years and Days

If you plan carefully, you can get to Mars in about seven months.

All the planets orbit the sun. It takes Earth 365 days to orbit the sun once. It takes Mars almost twice that long to orbit the sun. You'll want to head for Mars when it is in the part of its orbit that is closest to Earth. That will give you the shortest trip.

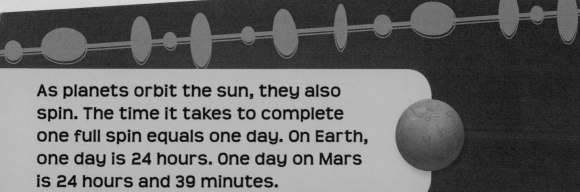

As planets orbit the sun, they also spin. The time it takes to complete one full spin equals one day. On Earth, one day is 24 hours. One day on Mars is 24 hours and 39 minutes.

Atmosphere

Seven months is a pretty long trip. You spend the time studying Mars. The planet is colder than Earth because it is farther from the sun. It also has a thin atmosphere, which means it doesn't trap very much heat.

The atmosphere of Mars is mostly carbon dioxide, the gas you breathe out. You brought a special suit that keeps out the cold and gives you oxygen to breathe.

EARTH

Moon

MARS

Phobos

Deimos

Size

You learn that the distance through Earth's middle is twice as big as that of Mars. And the distance through the middle of Mars is about twice as big as that of our moon. Mars has two very small moons, Phobos and Deimos.

Phobos and Deimos are tiny compared to Earth's moon.

Surface

At last, it's time to land! You step down onto the bright red-orange surface. You can see red clouds and red dust storms whirling about. Iron oxide gives the planet its special color. On Earth, you know this as rust!

You see that the surface of Mars is not all smooth. Look at those gullies. You remember they are valleys formed by melting snow.

Like Earth, Mars has a rock crust. It also has a rock mantle under the crust. The core of Mars is made of mostly iron and other elements, like Earth.

Gravity

When you land on Mars, you feel different. You bounce. You pick up a red rock and drop it. It takes longer to reach the ground than it would on Earth. That's because gravity here is about three times weaker than it is on Earth.

Small planets have weaker gravity than big, heavy ones.

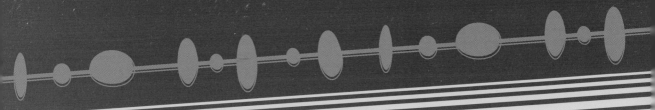

Tall Land

You see a huge mountain in the distance. You hike toward it to explore. It's so steep.

You measure its height. It's taller than Mount Everest, the highest mountain on Earth!

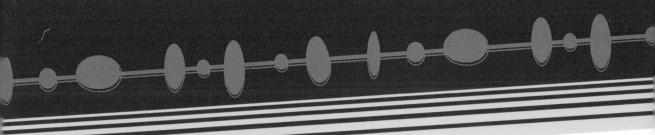

Volcanoes

You decide to hike up the mountain, and you find that it is actually a volcano. That's right! You remember that Mars has the biggest volcanoes in the solar system. The one you landed on is Olympus Mons. It is the tallest peak in the solar system.

Plains

You keep exploring. The land is flat for as far as you can see. These are the planet's northern plains. They are some of the flattest places in our solar system.

You do not see any water or other sign of life. Maybe if you jet south you will find something.

Canyons and Craters

You fly over the equator of Mars. There you see huge canyons. These canyons are called the Valles Marineris. They are many times deeper and wider than our own Grand Canyon. And they would stretch almost all the way across the United States.

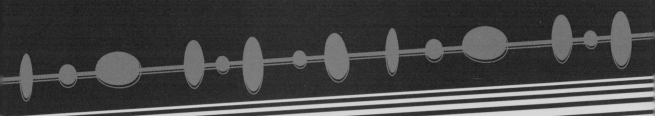

As you head south you see many sizes of craters. The craters were formed when meteorites slammed into the surface of the planet.

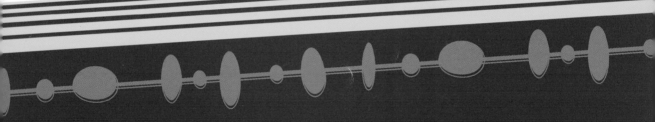

One large crater on Mars is Hellas Planitia. It is 1,400 miles (2,253 km) wide and almost six miles (10 km) deep. That's about half the size of the United States!

The South Pole

Your last stop is the south pole. This pole is made of frozen carbon dioxide, or dry ice. You take some of this ice home. You didn't find water ice. But scientists can still study the dry ice to learn more about Mars.

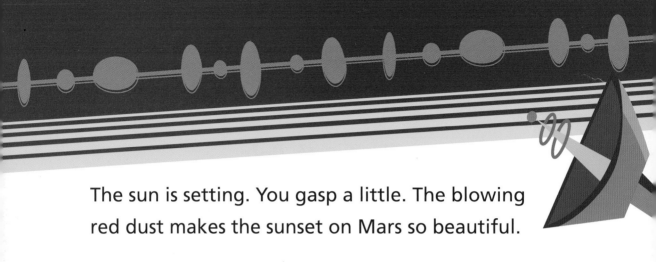

The sun is setting. You gasp a little. The blowing red dust makes the sunset on Mars so beautiful.

You head back to your spaceship for the night. Tomorrow you will continue to explore the amazing planet.

How Do Scientists Know about Mars?

People have watched Mars in the night sky since ancient times. In the early 1800s, Italian astronomer Giovanni Virginio Schiaparelli saw shapes that looked like canals on Mars. People soon believed that intelligent beings, or Martians, created the canals.

In the 1960s, the National Aeronautics and Space Administration (NASA) sent *Mariner 4*, *6*, and *7* to fly past Mars. The *Mariner* missions took photos of its craters. From those photos, scientists believed that Mars looked like Earth's moon. In 1976, the *Viking* spacecraft landed on Mars and took the first close-up pictures and soil samples of the planet. This mission did not find any life or canals made by living things.

In 1996, NASA launched the *Mars Pathfinder* and *Mars Global Surveyor*. *Mars Pathfinder* carried a robot that rolled down a ramp and moved among the rocks on Mars. It took photos and studied the rocks and soil. *Mars Global Surveyor* used advanced instruments to learn more about the surface of Mars. It made very good maps of the planet. In 2003, Mars passed closer to Earth than it had in 60,000 years. The Hubble Space Telescope took many great photos. In 2008, the *Phoenix Mars Lander* found water ice near the north pole of Mars.

The rover *Curiosity* is due to launch in late 2011. Its main purpose is to find out if Mars has ever supported life.

Mars Facts

Position: Fourth planet from sun

Distance from sun: 142 million miles (229 million km)

Diameter (distance through the planet's middle): 4,222 miles (6,795 km)

Length of orbit (year): Almost 2 Earth years

Length of rotation (day): 24 hours and 39 minutes

Moons: Phobos and Deimos

Gravity: Three times weaker than Earth's gravity

Words to Know

atmosphere—the layer of gases surrounding a planet.

core—the center of a planet.

crater—a dip in the ground shaped like a large bowl.

equator—an imaginary line around the center of a planet.

gas—a substance that spreads out to fit what it is in, like air in a tire.

gravity—the force that pulls a smaller object toward a larger object.

mantle—the part of a planet between the crust and the core.

meteorite—a chunk of rock from space that has crashed into a planet.

orbit—to travel around something, usually in an oval path.

solar system—a star and the objects, such as planets, that travel around it.

volcano—a mountain from which hot liquid rock or steam comes out.

Learn More

Books

Birch, Robin. *Mars*. New York: Facts on File, 2008.

Gibbons, Gail. *The Planets*. New York: Holiday House, 2007.

Goldsmith, Mike. *Solar System*. London: Kingfisher, 2010.

Web Sites

To learn more about Mars, visit ABDO Group online at **www.abdopublishing.com**. Web sites about Mars are featured on our Book Links page. These links are routinely monitored and updated to provide the most current information available.

Index